30 DAY DEVOTIONAL

SITTING WELL AT THE WELL

DR. JEANNE BROOKS

Copyright © 2017 Dr. Jeanne Brooks

All rights reserved. No part of this book may be used or reproduced by any means, graphic, electronic, or mechanical, including photocopying, recording, taping or by any information storage retrieval system without the written permission of the publisher except in the case of brief quotations embodied in critical articles and reviews This book is protected by copyright laws of the United States of America. This book may not be copied or reprinted for commercial gain or profit. Unless otherwise indicated, all Scripture quotations are taken from the Holy Bible, New Living Translation, copyright © 1996, 2004, 2007, 2013 by Tyndale House Foundation. Used by permission of Tyndale House Publishers, Inc., Carol Stream, Illinois 60188. All rights reserved.

www.ElaniPublishing.com

ISBN-13:978-1981547265

ISBN-10:1981547266

Forward

The Neurobiology of Sitting at The Well, Receiving, Restoring, and Renewing

The mission of my ministry is to help people to learn to "sit well at The Well." This concept is basically the idea of the significance of receiving the love of Christ in such a way that it restores us and renews us so we then are able to sit with others as they are receiving, being restored and renewed. However, to sit with others, we must first sit. It is in this act of sitting that we find peace. There is a neurological phenomenon of peace, but there is also the neurological phenomenon of anxiety and fear that can sometimes overpower our neurological peace. The act of sitting at the Well is an act of finding that neurological peace. To get that neurological peace that surpasses all understanding one must first find peace with the Lord for it is only the Lord that can settle us from our fears and shame. It is in the act of drawing closer to Him that settles our fears and shame. He is the one who can calm our anxious spirit. That anxiousness that comes from our experiences of shame and guilt. The act of sitting at The Well receiving the living water from our savior has the ability to wash over all the shame, guilt, and fear that we become riddled with.

Neurologically there is a profound significance of the act of sitting and focusing on our Saviors ability to wash us clean from our shame as compared to living in fear and shame. Neurologically it takes a far higher level of thinking and concentrating on the truths of our Savior's ability to wash us clean. It takes far greater intellectual ability. This higher cortex, this ability to reason, this ability to logically think through truths and create long-lasting loving relationships is an ability that God created just for us. He created it for us so we could come to know Him at a deep, loving level that also requires the ability to hold firm to His truths.

This act of sitting at The Well, receiving the love of our Savior and focusing on His truths, requires us to be active in our frontal cortex area of the brain, as compared to being stuck in our limbic system. The limbic system is the reactive area of the brain. This area of the brain is the part of the brain that has been referred to as the fight or flight system. The limbic system is also known as the "go" area, the area of the brain that is responsible for a very quick reaction that protects us from harm or danger. The limbic system is a great system when there is true danger but not so good when it is merely perceived danger.

The highly stressed or traumatized brain can misread external signals as danger, setting in motion a very quick reaction without much logic to counteract the shame that is driving the reaction. It is amazing how shame affects the brain. Shame is the belief that there is something innately bad/wrong with us. Shame can define us and define how we relate to one another. Shame is the result of what has happened to us and/or directly related choices we make. Guilt, as opposed to shame, is an emotion that warns us that what we are doing is wrong. Shame is a state of being that says who we are is wrong. Guilt guides us to adjust and change, shame guides us to cower and hide.

Shame drives the limbic system to perceive danger where there is none, setting the entire neurological system to "go" as if there is danger. When we are operating out of this "go" system, we are most certainly in a fight or flight mode. Responding to all that is around us as if we must run or fight. If in this neurological loop we are unable to sit at The Well, we are not responding to others well. Therefore, we are not sitting at The Well adequately. Remember, we are in a "go" mode that will cause us to fight or flight. Who wants to sit with someone who is in a fight or flight mode?

Therefore, it is imperative that we first sit at The Well with our Savior allowing Him to settle us. We need to allow Him to settle our "go" part of a brain and have Him show us how not to react to one another by fighting or running. Sitting with Him, looking into His loving eyes, allows us to focus on His truth, the truths of who He is and how He came to show us how much He loves us. It allows us to focus on how to love others as He loves us.

Sitting at The Well causes us to focus on these truths and helps us get out of the limbic system. It settles us and causes us not to want to run or fight. Sitting at The Well, breathing in His love, settles that limbic system allowing us to move into our logical, emotion-regulating brain. Receiving His love and letting it wash over us allows us to feel calmer. The calmer we feel, the more we can focus on whom He really is. The more we focus on who He really is, reminding ourselves of His truths in the Bible and in our lives the calmer we are. The more we sit with Him breathing in all of who He was and is, the less fear and shame we feel. Focusing on the truth that there is no guilt and no shame that is bigger than the cross. His death covered all that has happened to us or that we have done. There is not one thing that the cross cannot heal.

He took it all to the cross carrying it to the grave and not one thing is too big for the cross. Focusing on this, spending time in the word, acknowledging that His truths cover it all, and praising and worshiping Him helps us get out of that limbic system loop of shame, fear, and anxiety. Sitting, breathing it all in neurologically helps us out of our "go" brain and allows us to get into the higher cortex region of the relational brain where we no longer are reactive to the things around us. Instead, we are resting on His truths receiving His love.

In the receiving of His love, allowing ourselves to be present in the relational higher cortex region of our brain where logic and emotional regulation exist, we are far better able to reveal who He is to others. When we are emotionally regulating and focusing on truths of Him then we are far better able to sit well at The Well with others. In sitting well with others, it allows for a renewal of who we are to be as a church, a body of believers. A body of believers who love God first and love others secondly, are no longer riddled with self-deprecating and self-preservative behaviors that push others away.

However, beware; there is an enemy that has been working overtime to keep us captive in the limbic system. This enemy wants us stuck in shame and fear. He wants us to react to one another in hostility, judgment, and isolation to one another so we cannot meet Jesus at The Well. The devil wants to hold us hostage in the reactive brain, believing his lies and doubting God. The enemy entraps and isolates us. He keeps us in the dark causing us to be afraid of the light, the truth. The enemy wants us to believe that we are our shame and God's love is not for us. The devil wants us to believe his lies and doubt others. The enemy wants us to believe our brothers and sisters are our enemies. The enemy stimulates us to react to one another with hostility and fear. He has created many different avenues that drive us to this reactive area of the brain. The enemy uses divisive measures to cause us to doubt one another triggering our shame so we stay in the cyclical nature of reactivity, fighting or running from one another with little time to slow down and reason through truths. This inability to stay focused on logic keeps us emotionally unregulated, reacting very impulsively with one another. The enemy is causing our thoughts to go round and round the anxious, agitated cycle of distrust and animosity.

Nevertheless, our Savior is at The Well waiting patiently. He wants to offer us the living water that washes away all doubts and fears to help us focus on Him, His love, and His truths that will settle us. We just need to take the time to come to The Well to sit. Sit and Receive. Receive and be restored. Be restored and renewed. So that we may in turn be used to help others be restored and renewed.

Day 1

My God

I am perplexed and overwhelmed with the fact that Moses was unable to enter the promise land because he struck a rock two times instead of speaking to the rock. In Numbers 20:8, God told Moses, "You and Aaron must take the staff and assemble the entire community. As the people watch, speak to the rock over there, and it will pour out its water. You will provide enough water from the rock to satisfy the whole community and their livestock......Moses and Aaron assembled the people and he said, 'Listen you rebels! Must we bring you water from this rock?' Moses then struck the rock twice."

At first glance, it seems so harsh to say because Moses did not do exactly as God had commanded he would not get to see the promise land. This really has stuck with me. First, I think of how harsh that sounds and how that is not the God I have come to know and love. I do not want to think of a God that is so unforgiving that He would derail the only man He ever personally spoke to and guided through the dessert to rescue His people. The God I have grown to know and love is a forgiving God one with mercy and grace. I have been having a hard time reconciling this God with the Old Testament God. The Old Testament God who tells His people to "kill them all" and to "leave nothing behind", and who is very quick to anger and frustration. At least that is what it seems at first glance.

At first glance, I want to discount the Old Testament God. He is the one that kills everyone off in a flood. He is the same one who destroys two cities and turns a woman into a pillar of salt.

SITTING WELL AT THE WELL

The Old Testament God rules with an iron fist. At least it seems so at first glance. What did Moses do that was so bad? Why take away the promise land from him? Why cause him to wander for 40 years in the dessert only to die there? I want to focus on the loving, merciful God that pours grace upon me, not the God who asks me to do something and expects me to do it His way. I want to be able to make my mistakes, wander aimlessly in my own direction without consequences so that I can freely and COMFORTABLY come back to Him falling right back in place. However, that is not the God of Moses.

God very specifically asked Moses to tell the rock to pour out the water, but instead, Moses, out of anger and frustration of the people he was leading, struck the rock two times. Although God had instructed him a time earlier to strike a rock and water will flow, this time God wanted him to "speak to the rock". This has really troubled me. Moses "essentially" did what was asked of him. From my vantage point, he just got a few things wrong, but the end result was the same. Wasn't it? I am forced to look at how many times I have made adjustments to the rules but the end result being the same. What is so wrong with adding a little of me in the equation? God did create me. He knows me. Wouldn't He factor in the "Jeanne Factor"? Why wouldn't He factor in the "Moses Factor"?

God said to Moses, "Because you did not trust me enough to demonstrate my holiness to the people of Israel, you will not lead them into the land I am giving them!" He told Moses, "because you did not trust me". Wow, that is powerful! Then I think, well, Sarah certainly did not exhibit trust in the Lord to provide what He promised. In fact, she laughed and then decided that maybe God needed her help to complete this promise. She gave Abraham her maidservant (Genesis 16:1). In spite of this blatant mistrust, God still followed through with His promise and gave Sarah her own son. Sarah was able to realize her promise even though she brought in the "Sarah Factor" and tried her way. What did Moses do so wrong that he was denied the promise land?

God said, "Because you did not trust me enough *to demonstrate my holiness to the people of Israel*, you will not *lead them* into the land I am giving you." Wow! God had chosen Moses to demonstrate who God is to His people. The people who kept forgetting who God was. The people who wanted an idol to worship when Moses was gone too long talking to God. The people that were so enculturated by the pagan gods of the Egyptians God asked Moses to represent Him to these people. God wanted to use Moses to be a reflection of who God is. He wanted to reveal His mighty awesomeness to these people through Moses. However, when Moses allowed his own flesh of frustration, anger, and hostility to get in the way, the people saw Moses and his power of frustration and anger instead God's blessings of water.

God's instructions were to "speak to the rock". In 1 Kings 19:12, Elijah heard the "sound of a gentle whisper" and it was God. This was after a "mighty windstorm", "an earthquake", and "a fire". God was in none; He was in the "gentle whisper". Although God is a mighty, mighty God, he also can command the earth with His gentle whisper. As I reflect on that, I realize how powerful a gentle whisper can be in the midst of great storms. That gentle whisper can calm a storm. Makes me reflect on Jesus when He said "Silence! Be still!" to the waves on the sea of Galilea (Mark 4:39). God does not need a lot of flash to reveal Himself. God did not need nor did He want Moses to reveal his own anger, but to reveal God's provision. He wanted

Moses to not only to reveal His provisions but reveal it in a way that could absolutely not be denied a heavenly way. To "speak" to a rock and tell it to provide water can only be explained by the supernatural.

Instead, Moses was so frustrated with the people he was leading that he allowed his anger to dictate his actions. Although he was doing what God asked, he also was letting his anger in. His anger affected his ability to witness God's true power. When I reflect on that, I must ask myself how often have I allowed my anger and frustration at others "because they were not acting as Christians should". How often have I used hostile language to quote God's truths? How often have I self-righteously stood arguing my opinion as if it was right and using God as my defender? How often have I sat piously believing because I have a relationship with God that my anger and frustration are justified and can be exhibited? When I act in these ways, how does it affect the receiver's view of whom God is and how God can change them, direct them, and guide them? Does my display of my frustration guide the watchers of my behavior closer to my God or farther away? Is my behavior revealing the Old Testament God more than the New Testament God who had a plan all along?

My God is both the Old Testament and the New Testament God. My God is strong and mighty. In addition, He will discipline His children. His discipline sometimes might seem harsh on this side of eternity, but it is full of mercy and grace when looking at it from an eternal perspective. From an eternal perspective, Moses not getting to walk into the promise land does not seem so harsh anymore. Joshua, Moses' replacement, did not get to just walk in the promise land and settle it. He and his armies had to do a lot of fighting. They had to conquer the land. With

God's help, they seized regions of land one by one. It was not an easy task and there were many battles to be fought. Moses was freed from that. He was freed and was able to find rest with His Heavenly Father after 40 years of wandering. Not only was he able to find rest with His Heavenly Father, Moses was one of only two that got to be standing with Jesus as He was transformed in front of Peter, James, and John (Matthew 17:1-3), "Suddenly Moses and Elijah appeared and began talking with Jesus (3)".

From an eternal perspective, Moses got the jackpot. He got to go home and see everything from a far better vantage point. As I reflect on this, I can reconcile this mighty God who does have an iron fist and a gentle loving heart. I can reconcile that the Old Testament God is the same as the New Testament God. He is mighty. He does get angry. He does discipline. He does crush, and He does forgive. He does love. He shows mercy. He is faithful. He is all this and much more. I cannot not just rely on His mercy without knowing His commands. I cannot rely on His grace without knowing He does want it His way. I cannot rely on His forgiveness and justify doing it my way. His way is perfect my way is faulty. His way draws others into Him while my way distracts others from Him. His way offers salvation while my way offers condemnation. His way offers eternity while my way offers damnation.

Day 2

The Silence in the Hurriedness

One day I was busy going from one Bible study to the next. I was doing for God what I was certain He needed me to do. I found myself rushed and remembered I needed napkins and plates for the snacks provided at the study. I saw some really cute plates and napkins that matched. I read the first several lines written on the napkins, and it sounded so sweet. I grabbed them and ran on. It was not until I was in the midst of Bible study and all the women had their cute little plates and matching napkins, that I realized the last few lines on the napkin. They were not sweet and certainly not edifying. Oh, the problems that come in a busy life! Even when our intentions are pure, the outcome can fall short. At that moment, I was reminded of a lesson on soul keeping and how our souls have difficulty finding peace in a hurried life. In 1 Kings 19:11-13, Elijah is brought to realize that God is not always found in great winds or earthquakes, He is often found in stillness. In thinking of these two concepts, I came to understand that I am unable to hear God in the whirlwind of my hurried life, I best hear God in the stillness of the day. For this day, I will find a time to sit, be still, and listen.

Day 3

How am I Responding

Reading in Jonah makes me really think of my prejudices. Jonah ran from God's request because of his distain and prejudice towards the people of Nineveh (Jonah 1). I must ask myself how often do I run from God, not truly loving others as He would call me to do. A prejudice is defined as harm or injury that results from an action or a judgement. God's word is very clear that we are not to judge. He judges, and we are to love. I find myself pondering on what I really mean when I speak of loving the person but hating the sin. Is hating the sin causing me to be perceived as condemning? Does "hating" the sin cause me to look prejudice? Alternatively, am I really being prejudice, hating the sin, and really not even liking the person? If I am not really liking the person, then how honest am I about loving the person? Am I really just truly judging and condemning? For I am not the one to condemn. God has authority to condemn. God is in the business of saving not condemning, redeeming not judging. Jonah wanted God to condemn, but God wanted to redeem. Jonah ran, but God wanted to use Him to save. As He did with Jonah, He may desire to use me to go and share of God's truth in such a way that will allow those lost in the darkness of sin to see light.

Jonah was so caught up in his own dislike of the people of Nineveh that he did not want to do what God called him to do. Jonah failed to recognize what an honor it can be to be called into God's work, loving people, sharing God's truth, and allowing God to use him to bring them out of the darkness into the light. I must ask myself, how am I like Jonah? Why is it that I am not willing to sit with sinners and to love them where they are? Why am I not allowing God to pour His love and truth through me in such a way that it draws the sinner close to God so God can redeem them? Why am I more comfortable sitting back talking about how the world has fallen into darkness, our society has succumbed to lies, and our culture has declined into self-seeking, self-righteous ways? Why do I self-righteously look upon the sinner as if the sinner is doing something far worse then I?

I weighs sin, as if one sin is worse than another sin. God does not. I compare my sin to others as if that makes me better. God looks upon me in the same way He looks upon those I am judging. He loves us all. Jonah was very certain that if he went to Nineveh and did as God had requested, the people would come to repent, and God would forgive. Jonah did not want God forgiving Nineveh. Jonah wanted God to place a judging hand upon Nineveh condemning them to eternity in hell (Jonah 4). The reality of Jonah's true heart condition really has caused me to look at my own heart condition. Are there groups of people or persons in my life that I am so prejudice against or so full of hate that I am unable to forgive or unable to love in a way that could bring the truth of God into their lives? Am I like Jonah, refusing to love my enemy as God loved me.

I was God's enemy at one time, walking in sin despising His truth and living in darkness. The problem was I did not realize I was in the dark. I did not realize how I was rejecting the truth. I certainly did not realize that as an idolater of things of this world I was acting as an enemy to God, opposing all He has done for me. I am very grateful that He chose not to forsake me as He chose not to forsake Nineveh. I am so glad that He went to great means to rescue me and reveal His truth to me as He did with Nineveh. I still, however, ponder on Jonah and his response to it all. He was really mad at God for saving Nineveh (Jonah 4:3). He was so filled with self-righteousness and hate that he could not fully grasp the grace and mercy of God. He could not see how God really wants that revealed to all.

I must go back to the question. Who are the Nineveh in my life? Who are the persons in my life that I am failing to show grace and mercy? How can I better love the person? How can I become a friend to sinners and loved them where they are rather than waiting for them to be better, be cleaner, and sinless? I must admit, I am guilty of judging others and praying for others but not really loving them, sitting with them, and walking with them. Instead, I pray and wait until they come into where I am. I am essentially waiting for them to clean up their life enough for me to sit with them. Sometimes others' lives are just too messy for me to sit with. That is the sad truth. Jonah may have seen Nineveh as just too messy of a place to go to; his judgement was that they did not deserve God's grace and mercy. My actions suggest a similar stance. If I am not willing to become friends to sinners, then I might as well spend some time in the belly of a whale. Sitting in my own stench of sin, recognizing that my sin in God's eyes is no different from "those peoples sin".

I then must ask myself why I will not become a friend of sinners. Jesus was. In fact, Jesus is my friend. He is a friend of a sinner. He loves me in the midst of my sin. He does not condemn me. He does not stay away from me. He does not just pray for me. He does not wait for me to clean up my act. He is with me always even in the midst of my sin. Jesus does nothing in response to my sin that causes harm. He responds to my sin in such a loving way that causes me to want not to sin. Jesus shows no prejudice towards me. He shows me just love. A love that surpasses all understanding. A love that is healing. A love that is life changing. A love that washes me clean of sin. He does that for me daily and all day long. Never once does He condemn me. He only lovingly convicts me. This conviction is so gentle and loving, it causes me to surrender it all to him so he can continue to change me, grow me, and remake me. All so, I may *know* His love and give it to others.

He says love my enemies (Matthew 5:43-48). He says love others as I have loved you (John 13:34). He says feed the hungry, quench the thirsty, clothe the naked, and give respite to the homeless (Matthew 35:37-40). There are sinners around me hungry for the truth. Am I filling them with God's joy? There are sinners out there thirsty for life. Am I filling them with God's love? There are sinners out there naked and ashamed. Am I clothing them in God's peace? There are sinners out there without a home. Am I providing shelter with God's gentleness and kindness? Alternatively, am I succumbing to my own sinful desires meeting them with hostility, and judgment?

Day 4

Are we Hungry Enough Yet?

God does not use His people and their strength to show others how strong and mighty they are. God uses His people's weaknesses to show the world how strong and mighty He is. The question comes are we there yet? Are we at the end of our rope of our own self-sufficiency to give it all to God? Are we at a place of complete repentance to recognize that it is not in our ability to turn things around? Have we come to the end of the line and recognize the cliff of abyss? Are we truly hungry enough with no other place to look but up? Years ago, there was an advertisement for a fast food chain with a catch term, "where is the beef?" Are we looking in all the wrong places for the meat of the matter, the solution for the fix?

Everywhere I turn, I hear people say how tired and weary they are. Jesus said, "Come to me, all of you who are weary and carry heavy burdens, and I will give you rest. Take my yoke upon you. Let me teach you, because I am humble and gentle at heart, and you will find rest for your souls. For my yoke is easy to bear, and the burden I give is light" (Matthew 11: 27-30). Jesus is referencing that because of Him we are no longer under the laws that we cannot follow anyway. If we truly follow Him, we will be light in spirit. Throughout the Bible God warns against us following our own desires to do "for Him" and instead to do with Him. Psalm 127:1-2, "unless the Lord builds a house the work of the workers is wasted. Unless the Lord protects a city, guarding it with sentries will be no good. It is useless for you to work so hard from morning to night, anxiously working for food to eat; for God gives rest to his loved ones." We toil all day for not. We can have a tendency to think what we are doing "for Him" is worthy. Yet in the doing, we grow weary and in our weariness, we grow anxious and agitated. In our anxiousness and agitation, we become bitter and bewildered as to why God is not strengthening us, protecting us, and causing comfort for us.

Isaiah 58: 2-4, "Yet they acted so pious! They came to the temple every day and seemed delighted to learn about me. They acted like a righteous nation that would never abandon God's laws. They ask me to take action on their behalf, pretending they want to be near me. 'We have fasted before you!' they say. 'Why aren't you impressed? We have been very hard on ourselves, and you don't even notice!' 'I will tell you why!' I respond. 'It is because you are fasting to please yourselves. Even while you fast, you are oppressing your workers. What good is fasting when you keep on fighting and quarrelling?' It seems to me that we are a nation that is filled with very self-sufficient people working very hard for our own comfort and define the comfort as God's blessing upon us. Even the work we do under the guise of "doing for Him" truly is likely work that makes us feel good about ourselves. It feels good to do good, but what if doing good means self-sacrificing? Jesus says His burden is light. He does not say it is easy. However, I think maybe we have it backwards. We take on burdens that are heavy and cause us to be weary, but in a sense, they are easy. Easy in the sense that I can always go back to my comfortable home, sleep in my comfortable bed, and enjoy the fellowship of those that I am comfortable around. I am never too far from my comfort.

When I become uncomfortable, I do what I need to do to get back into my comfort. I rely on my own abilities for comfort and believe I deserve comfort for all the good I have done. Does that sound familiar? It seems to me we are a Nation of comfort seekers, and we rely on our own abilities to get back to comfort believing we deserve this comfort. We are a nation that has been fortunate enough to be able to experience a great deal of comfort. Our homes are air-conditioned. We have indoor plumbing and plenty of bathrooms for all. Our cars have cruise control. Our grocery stores are stocked. There are fast food restaurants on every corner (or at least a Starbucks). If we need anything, it is at the click of our fingers, and we can have same day delivery. Most of us do not know what it is to be hungry, really truly hungry to where we do not know when and if another meal is coming our way. For most of us, if we have experienced true hunger it is by choice through fasting. With fasting, we know there is an end so even in our discomfort we know comfort is coming our way.

We are so comfortable that even when we give until it hurts, we know the hurting will soon be over. Very few in this nation understand the meaning of true sacrifice, sacrifice that is asked of us. Few understand what it is to work with God. We are too busy working for God without really understanding God does not need us to work for Him. He does want us to work with Him. We toil and toil, working our fingers to the bone and growing weary all "for Him" and "His glory". If it really is all for Him and His glory, why are we exhibiting such fleshy fruits such as sexual immorality, impurity, lustful pleasures, idolatry, sorcery, hostility, quarreling, jealousy, outbursts of anger, selfish ambition, dissension, division, envy, drunkenness, wild parties, and other sibs like these? Why are Christians no different from the rest of the world when looking at the statistics of divorce or pornography addiction? Why are brothers and sister using social media to fight a quarrel about doctrine and who is voting for whom? Why are our children going with us to church on Sundays watching us praise our Heavenly Father, only to see us go into fits of anger on Mondays? Why is it that we so easy condemn others for the speck in their eyes while clearly missing the log in our own? Are we those pious people that Isaiah warns about?

If we are, have we come to recognize it? Have we come to the end of our rope of self-sufficiency? Are we hungry for deliverance yet? I have heard it said a few times, "we might just pull ourselves out of this mess we are in". On the other hand, "I do not know what we are going to do about the mess we are in". Both statements, weather hope filled or hopeless, are self-reliant statements. We are at a place in our nation that we can do nothing to change the tides of this self-destruction. If we are really truly honest with ourselves, not one person, government, or election can truly turn the tides of the devastation that is before us. However, there is no despair in knowing that. That is a good place to be, knowing that there is nothing we can do because then and only then will we be at the best place. The best place is on our knees looking up at He who is the only true answer and only true solution. Are we hungry enough? Are we there yet? If not, we will be!

Day 5

God's Victory

I love what I read this morning in Beth Moore's *David, Seeking a Heart Like His (2010)*. She writes, "God often gives us victory that requires blood, sweat, and tears....When He can bring about a victory and strengthen us all at the same time, He's likely to do it" (p. 93). Beth goes on to suggest that not only does God's type of victory often require our hard work, but also His victory is not defined as the world would define it, complete annihilation of our enemy. God is not so concerned as to the end result of the battle; His concern is the end result of His people. His desire is for us to grow strong in Him. Today, I will not judge my success by the final outcome of the day, but instead but by my ability to accept God's peace and joy regardless of my accomplishments.

Day 6

Are we Salt or Cayenne Pepper?

As I was driving to work one day, I heard an advertisement about the new movie being released, Noah, on the Christian radio. Within the endorsement, there was a seemingly heartfelt thank you to Paramount Pictures for producing this story. I am also thankful that once again there will be a story on the big screen depicting how great our God is. I love the fact that just recently the movie, Son of God, was released and record numbers came to see it. In addition to that, a TV mini-series entitled The Bible received great viewership last Fall. What awesome opportunities for doors to be opened for us as believers to witness to those who do not understand the good news. However, I do find it disconcerting that I hear amongst believers and read on the social media sites such as Twitter and Facebook how believers are arguing about the Biblical accuracy or how Hollywood has watered down the stories. I myself was amongst some that wanted to criticize The Bible mini-series when it first came out because it did not have all the stories in it that I deemed significant. I was gently reminded that it would be very challenging to get every detail in such a series. Then I was asked, "Isn't it good, though, that those who know very little or nothing of God's love and His plan of redemption get to see it played out in such a way?" That question humbled me. I realized that my own self-righteousness was a way that the devil could use me to discredit the truths that were being told, and that any debate I might want to throw out there to reveal my knowledge could just be noise that would create interference for that lost sheep that really needed to hear some good news. James asks, "What is causing the quarrels and fights among you?...Don't speak evil against each other, dear brothers and sisters. If you criticize each other, then you are criticizing God's law" (James 4:1-11). I think of James' question today and the significance of it in relation to the current condition of our Nation. How in the world can I truly be salt and light to this world if I am busy arguing amongst other believers about what God's word truly means and how to communicate it to others? Salt is a seasoning used to bring out the best flavor of a food. Is my arguing exposing the best of God, His love? Alternatively, is my arguing more like cayenne pepper, drowning out the flavor and making it too hot to digest? The truth is "No eye has seen no ear has heard no mind has conceived what God has prepared for those who love Him" (1 Cor 2:9). Anything I try to explain outside of what the Bible says is mere human conjecture. Instead of spending time arguing, I think I will better spend my time. I will choose to love others as Jesus came and loved me proving to the world whose disciple I am (John 13:24).

Day 7

A Body Divided

We are a Church divided. We are divided between the concepts of love and truth. Love without truth is blind. Truth without love is judgmental. This division creates a body that is in constant turmoil and strife. We spend time arguing over godless matters (1 Timothy 4:7). The problem is when we are divided and arguing, we all have it wrong; one side is only half of the story. The full story is that God gave us Christ to reveal the truth about His love. When Jesus died and came back, He left us the Holy Spirit that is truth and love. John 14:17 states, "He is the Holy Spirit, who leads us into truth." Galatians 5:22 states, "But when the Holy Spirit controls our lives, He will produce this kind of fruit in us: love, joy, peace, patience, kindness, goodness, faithfulness, gentleness, and self-control."

When the focus is strictly on love, then we have the potential for loving others to death. The truth exists not for the purpose of judgment and condemnation; it exists to give us direction to God's loving kindness. Without the boundaries of truth, we will wander into dangerous territory. Territory that leads us farther and farther away from God's love. God's love is full of mercy and grace. God's love is healing. God's love renders nor shame. God's love is freeing. As someone who has lived in a full life of sin, I am painfully aware of the shame and fear sin creates in a life. Not because of God's truths but because of my distance from His love. Romans 1:21 states, "Yes, they knew God, but they wouldn't worship him as God or even give him thanks. And they began to think up foolish ideas of what God was like. The result was that their minds became dark and confused."

It was not the condemnation of His truth that caused me to be confused and in darkness. It was the lack of openly receiving and willingly receiving His love that kept me in the darkness. A child who is running from their mother is not lacking the loving arms of her embrace because she told her not to run. The child is not receiving the tender arms of mercy because she is running. Truth is truth, and we cannot run from it. Running from it just keeps us farther from it. However, truth without love is hurtful and destructive. A loving mother is not going to withhold her embrace when the child finally comes back. Nor is the child likely to come back if the mother is screaming how bad the child is for ignoring her love.

Nevertheless, sharing truth in love, just as Jesus did to the Samaritan woman (John 4), opens the heart of the person lost. Jesus did not stand upon a pulpit or even post on Facebook the sins that will render people to hell. He never pointed fingers or raised his voice at the lost, the sinners. Truth be told, the times he did get mad were at the Pharisees, the teachers of God's law. He got mad because they did a very poor job at representing His love. In the same light though, Jesus never left a sin filled situation without delivering loving truth. Jesus said to the woman caught in adultery, "Where are your accusers? Didn't even one of them condemn you?" "No Lord", she said. And Jesus said, "Neither do I. Go and sin no more." What a beautiful depiction of loving grace and mercy delivered in truth.

We are a church divided, arguing about ungodly things.

Day 8

A House Divided

Neurologically when the Corpus Callosum, a large bundle of fibers connecting the right brain to the left brain, is severed the individual suffers greatly. Essentially the person lives in a body divided. The right brain no longer is effectively communicating with the left brain. It seems to me as though The Church, the one built upon the corner stone of Jesus Christ, is divided. We are clearly a body divided. We are arguing amongst ourselves and condemning one another all the while losing our ability to witness to the lost. We are so busy shaming our brothers and sisters in Christ that we no longer look appealing to the lost. When I look at how my brothers and sisters in Christ use social media to speak against other brothers and sisters, I am saddened. Although I am often impressed with the rhetoric expressed by all sides, I am saddened that this discord is for all to see. I understand why outsiders may think we are foolish and why they question a belief system that is based on a book that not even the followers can agree on. Although the rhetoric is impressive and persuasive, it only leaves the lost even more confused and lost. Maybe that is why Jesus warned against this type of discourse. In Matthew 18:15, He warns the early church to correct one another privately or amongst believers.

I struggle even writing this because the reality is I am doing the same thing. Hence, I discourage any non-believer to not read this post for it will only confuse you. My words are meant to be read by my fellow brothers and sisters in Christ. I love how Paul shares with us the importance of spending time together, fellowshipping, meditating on the word, and encouraging and lifting one another in God's truths. It seems to me we have lost that important practice by staying far too busy doing rather than being. It is in this business that we have lost the art of relating. In losing the art of relating, we have lost the art of conversing. It is in the relating and conversing that we as fellow believers could learn to navigate the turbulent waters we are all entering into. Sadly, since we are so busy and social media is the place we have learned to communicate, this is the place we are choosing to relate and debate. Sadly, I believe choosing to use this form to air out the confusion only opens the door to validate non-believers' presumptions that the foundational truths in the Bible for which we stand upon are wishy-washy and fallible.

The rhetoric expressed is impressive because of the Biblical knowledge shared. The problem is this. If I can see and agree upon two completely opposing sides because of the Biblical truth expressed, then as believer, I have to choose to believe either both sides have great fallacy or the Bible has fallacy. As a believer, I choose to have faith in the Bible, not mankind. Therefore, I will choose to believe that regardless of how persuasive the argument is there must be some fault to it. As a believer, this is easy for me to digest because I know the imperfect nature of mankind. That is from a perspective of a believer. A nonbeliever sees mankind, themselves, as their own god. Therefore, the rhetoric expressed in open forum only goes to prove what they already believe, the Bible is fallible.

The body of 'The Church' (the Church of Jesus Christ) divided causes a house to be divided. A house divided is filled with turmoil and conflict. A house full of turmoil and conflict is not welcoming. In fact, a house that is full of turmoil and conflict is one that the lost are very likely to run from and not to. If I am lost, hurting, and alone, I am not likely going to go into a house for which the individuals inside are engaging in gossip, judgment, and ridicule. Jesus said, "Come to me, all of you who are weary and carry heavy burdens, and I will give you rest. Take my yoke upon you. Let me teach you, because I am humble and gentle at heart, and you will find rest for your souls" (Matthew 11:28-29). Paul writes, "We are His house, built on the foundation of the apostles and the prophets. And the cornerstone is Christ himself" (Ephesians 2:20). The original Church was one that called to the broken, weary, hurting, and lost, humbly inviting all that needed rest. I wonder if this public rhetoric offers that type of welcome to the lost and lonely.

As a family of believers, it is unrealistic to believe that we will agree upon all things. It is unrealistic to believe that in our flesh we will always be loving and kind. As with any family, there will be disagreements and challenges. However, as Jesus said, "If we have disagreement, if one has offended another, we should go to that person and talk it through." We should hammer out our discord amongst ourselves. In doing so, we can learn to grow in each other. We can begin sharpening and growing one another in our faith. We can learn to trust the heart of each other rather than judging the actions of each other. In doing so, we can become united and strong. We can begin acting and behaving as one body of believers. As a body of believers gathering together and going out witnessing to the world while radiating salt and light upon a bitter and dark world. If our house radiates this light, maybe it will be inviting to the lost, weary, and wounded. If we have a united house of worship, maybe more will come to worship.

As I wrote this, I found myself guilty on all accords. I believe we are all guilty. We have all bought into the divisiveness of the devils ploys and have been attending to the speck in each other's eyes rather than removing the log from our own. Because I am convicted, I posted this on social media the following prayer request:

I am in desperate need for prayer.

I am asking all my brothers and sisters in Christ to pray for me. I am very tired, weary, and scared. I can become so overwhelmed with the state of this world that I forget how big our God is. The Word encourages me not to grow weary for Christ carries my burdens and lightens my load, but my fear sometimes causes me to forget. The Word says fear not and pray about all things. However, my tiredness just causes me to grumble and complain of the current happenings. Not only am I finding myself grumbling and fearful, I'm finding myself judgmental and hurtful to you, my brothers and sisters in Christ. I find myself judging you when I am not in agreement with you about the happenings around me. I find myself becoming arrogant and prideful thinking I have far greater understanding of God's Word then you. I use the scripture that comes to my mind to support my pride and judgment. I forget that the enemy, the devil, can do that, use scripture to tempt me away from the Lord's promises. The devil can also use me to hurt you, my brother and sister in Christ. I easily forget the enemy is tricky; one of the devil's ploys is to create dissension. I need your prayers to not succumb to the Devils ploys of divisiveness when jealousy comes my way. When I see you doing something I think God wants me to do. I become jealous and then fall to judgment again. I need your prayers that God opens my eyes to the real enemy, the devil. I need your prayer that I will not use God's weapons of truth against my brothers and sisters but instead against the real enemy. I can so easily forget that this is not a battle between flesh and blood but a spiritual battle. I can so easily forget that you are my brothers and sisters and as God is rising me up in one direction, He may be rising you up in another. My pride and arrogance gets in the way, and I think that the direction God has me going is the direction you should go as well. Instead of encouraging and strengthening, I am judging and shaming. I forget to go to my knees to pray for you, my brother and sister. I succumb to fear rather than trust. I very quickly forget to trust God in your heart and His ability to guide you where He wants you. Sadly, I pride fully think it is my job to condemn you for what wrong I perceive in you. I am sorry that I am quick to judge and slow to pray. I am sorry that I choose gossip over coming to you as a sister and praying with you that God will join our hearts in His cause. My heart is burdened at the log in my eye. I am so sorry for addressing the speck in yours. Please pray God keeps me humble, yet bold. Please pray that in these trying times, I am given the strength to encourage and not tear down. Please pray that I stay united with my brothers and sister in Christ in these very trying times. That I stay firm in His mighty truths and that I stay committed to His army regardless if I agree with you or not. Please pray that I begin each daily battle on my knees praying for our unity in seeing things from an eternal perspective. Please forgive me for judgment I have had upon you. I love you all as my brothers and sisters, and I will fight this fight with you even when I do not agree with you. For I know our God will unite us all as we fight on our knees.

Day 9

Building Relationships

I remember well the night I first accepted and acknowledged Jesus as my Savior, choosing Him over the life I had been living. I remember feeling as though this encounter just might be life changing. I was hoping it would be, but not completely certain as to how. Funny, I also remember meeting my husband, Don, for the first time. Truth be told, I wondered if this encounter might be life changing, at least I hoped it would. When I first encountered Jesus and accepted that He definitely was a far better solution to my problems than anything I had attempted up to that point, I recognized something in Him that was intriguing, alluring, and worth pursuing. Not so different was my reaction to Don, I was intrigued. I was definitely attracted/allured to him and felt he might just be worth pursuing.

When I first met Jesus and accepted His invitation to join Him in His flock, I cannot say I knew Him, but I was definitely attracted to Him. I wanted what He promised, yet I *really* did not know Him. No different is the fact that when I first met Don, I did not really know him. I would have gladly accepted an invitation to join him for coffee or a dinner. I was certainly attracted to him and what the possibilities of getting to know him might offer, but I did not *really* know him. To come to know Don, I had to spend time with him. That first encounter with Don was merely that. The first encounter was a time that offered me a glimpse of who he was. To come to really know Don I had to purposely spend time with him, talking with him, walking with him, and listening to him. That was six years ago. Over the years, walking with him, talking to him, and listening to him has grown me in knowing him. The more I get to know, the more I want to know. However, the key is the purposeful commitment of spending time with him.

When I met Don, I was so intrigued by him I was afraid. I was afraid of the interest I had in him. The interest that may not be reciprocated. What a risk that would be. I also remember a fear in coming to Jesus. It was a different type of fear. The fear I experienced with Jesus was this overwhelming sense of respect, a respect of who He was. An awe-inspiring fear of having a sense that He was special in a way I had never known before. My fear of Don was that he might become special to me and that I would not become special to him. The way I dealt with these fears was talk to my friends about him. I wanted to learn about Don Brooks. I wanted to find out if he were a person I might be able to trust taking a risk with, a risk of becoming more intrigued with him. His friends, who were my friends, told me all the great things about him. They told me all the great things about him because they wanted me to risk it all so I would come to know Don. They wanted for me what they thought Don might be able to give me, companionship and possibly even love.

This awkward stage of getting to know Don was not so different then my getting to know Jesus. Because I was awe struck by His majesty, I depended on others to tell me whom He was. I attended church and listened to pastor's share of His love. I read books by many who professed His strength in their lives. I sang songs that professed His love and faithfulness. I heard repeatedly by others who He was and how He could be trusted. These persons shared this because they wanted me to have what they knew Jesus could give. My knowledge of my Lord and

Savior grew just as my knowledge of Don Brooks grew. The more I heard, the more I knew about. Problem is one does not grow in a relationship based off knowledge of. Intimacy does not come from knowing about, it comes from knowing. Knowing can only come with spending time with.

I know I had to have driven my friends absolutely crazy with all my questions about Don Brooks. We can certainly laugh now as to all the things I feared. I was not an easy egg to crack. My friends would contest to that. The issue was that I just was certain Don Brooks would not be interested in me. When he did show some interest, I was certain he would not come to like me or want to spend time with me ongoing. When he did seemingly enjoy his time with me and continued to pursue more time I was certain he could not grow to love me. I felt completely unworthy of love from a man like Don Brooks.

My walk with the Lord, my Savior, was not so different. The more I heard about Him and who He was in others' lives the more certain I became that He would not and could not love me as He does others. Yes, He was my Savior. That was never in question, but that had more to do with Him feeling sorry for me as if I was the last one left to be picked on a team. His love for me was more out of pity than an unconditional wash clean, made new, kind of love. I listened and heard of all the things He had done for others but somehow just did not believe that was possible for me. This was all because I knew of Him and heard about Him, but I did not know Him yet.

At some point in my growing with Don, I stopped asking questions about him but instead spent more time with him. At some point in my growing with Don, I stopped looking to others for help to discern who he was in my life. Instead, I started looking more to Don for that clarity. When I stopped looking to others to help me clarify who he should be in my life and instead looked to him, I grew to trust his love and who he was in my life. I also found that who Don is in my life is different then who he is in other people's life, so to look to them to help me understand him is quit futile. The relationship Don and I have is different from the relationship he has with others, so how he is with me has a different spin to it. Even though he is the same man in all situations, how he is with me is different from how he is with someone else. He and I have a different dance. What is so wonderful, refreshing, and life changing for us is I have found that Don does love me. He loves me with a beautiful love that is kind and worth trusting. Regardless of what I thought he would see in me, Don Brooks sees a woman he loves, and I love that. I now know that none of this would have come to fruition if I had not stopped going to others to learn more about Don. It is only because I chose to risk it all and spend time with Don, allowing our relationship to grow, that it was able to grow into a place of me realizing his ability to love even me.

This is true about Christ too. There is no way to come to know Christ without purposely spending time with Him. I can spend all my time with others learning about His love, or I can spend time with Him receiving His love. I can hear all day long of a love so deep and so wide that it is beyond understanding, but all that will do is cause me to understand even less and question even more. In order to build a relationship with the Lord, I must spend time with Him. Just like the development of my relationship with my husband, it required me to spend time with him. I needed to come to know him and to come to trust him. It is the same with Jesus. Jesus calls us to Him. Jesus desires us to know Him not just know of Him. Jesus wants to walk with us and talk with us. We just need to join Him.

In addition, the sustaining of a relationship requires continued purposeful time spent with one another. Don and I married December 28, 2010. It would not be much of a marriage today if after we married I stopped spending time with him. The relationship would not grow if I only checked in with him once a week for about an hour. The relationship would falter if I spent far more time with others then with him. He would not feel loved by me if I put everyone else in front of the giving of my time. I do believe Don would feel very neglected if I kept putting my time with him on the back burner to take care of all the other things in my life. He would feel even worse if the only time I really checked in with him was when I needed something or I was sick. Relationships really do not flourish when there is no time invested. My relationship with Christ, the most important relationship in my life, requires me to give Him my time, to sit with Him, walk with Him, talk to Him, and listen. My relationship with Christ only grows if I show up and relate with Him. He is always there waiting. I just have to come in. The more I come, the more I grow in Him. Then more I want to come even more. First, I must come.

Day 10

Balance verses Starting Point

There is a lot of talk about the importance of balance. A balanced budget, a balanced diet, and a balanced life are a few examples. I have found myself trying to find that "balance" and have found great difficulty in rectifying that balance as I walk closer to God. When I left Texas years ago, I struggled with the world's call to balance family and work. Yet I was leaving my family. The Bible says one will leave brothers, sisters, mothers and fathers behind to follow Him (Matthew 19:29). When I have grown worn and weary following Abba, I think of what the world says about stress management. Then I read of Jesus and His disciples trying to get away from the crowd but the crowd followed (Matthew 14:13-16). When I think of what the world says of the importance of having a life, I think of Jesus stating we must lose our life (Matthew 10:39). It seems to me the scales for which the world balances life issues keep on being readjusted. Therefore, I am not so sure if defining a healthy life style is best balanced by the world's scales. Instead of determining my "accomplishments" in a day or instead of looking for validation by the scales of the world, I first ask myself what was my starting point. Did I start the day in my Father's arms asking Him to empty me of me and fill me with Him? Did I start the day seeking His purpose for me in this day rather than determining my agenda? Did I start the day asking Him to fill me up with His love so I may love others? Did I start the day resting in His assurances? Then at the end of the day, I land back in His arms. Even if by the world standards I strike out, I can hear Him say good job faithful servant. At that point, I can find rest believing by His standards it was a home run and I am back to home base, my starting point. That is a balanced life I can live with.

Day 11

Discernment

Discernment is the ability to judge well. Discerning God's voice is the ability to determine it is He that is calling. In determining God's voice one must know God, His Word, and His loving character. God will never contradict His Word nor ask you to act outside of God's love. God calls us into action not because He needs us, but because He wants to use us. To be called into action one must be able to discern God's calling and to discern His calling one must know His Word. We are always at risk of falling into a self-driven calling, under the guise of God's will. In 2 Samuel 24, David calls for a census, "go and count the people of Israel and Judah" (v. 1b). I Chronicles 21 states, "Satan rose up against Israel and caused David to take a census of the people of Israel" (v. 1). God had ordered a census to be taken in Number 1-2 Aaron and Moses were told by the Lord to take a census for the purpose of determining the number of abled body men to serve in the military to conquer the Promise Land. The Israelites had grown so in number and census was needed. David's calling of a census was based on his pride and a desire to glory in the size of his army and the power he had from it. David was beginning to rely on himself and the size of his army rather than relying on God. God desires for His power to be revealed through us, "We use God's weapons, not worldly weapons, to knock down stronghold…." (2 Corinthians 10:4a). God's mighty weapons are available to us to knock down the devils strongholds. Yet, the devil is always lurking trying to deceive, distract, and divert. Judges 7 reveals God's power and strength through the victory He gave Gideon after reducing his army from 32,000 to 300. Gideon's faith in the Lord is in complete opposition to David's pride. Gideon finds his strength in the Lord and shows his faith by reducing his army to a mere 300 while David attempts to define his power by his large army. Gideon was able to discern God's calling and accepted it. David fell to the sin of pride. He was led by Satan and a three day plague came upon Israel (2 Samuel 24:15).

Day 12

David Honored Saul

Reading through 1 Samuel is an interesting journey of intrigue and suspense with a villain, Saul, constantly seeking to kill the hero, David. They first meet when David is but a boy, and Saul is immediately taken by the young man, especially when David tells King Saul, "Don't worry about that Philistine [the giant Goliath] I'll fight him!" From the moment David conquered the giant with only a sling shot and a stone, it became evident David was a gifted warrior. "Whatever Saul asked David to do, David did successfully. So Saul made him commander over the men of war, an appointment that was welcomed by the people and Saul's officers alike" (1 Samuel 18:5). Because of David's skill, the people began singing, "Saul has killed his thousands and David ten thousand" (1 Samuel 18:7).

Saul's admiration for David quickly turned to jealousy. It was an insane jealousy that led to Saul's insatiable desire to kill David. Every step David took, Saul was close by plotting to end his life. Saul's thirst for David's blood was unquenchable. Saul's obsession with killing David became pathological and unstoppable. Saul was so arrogant that he could not allow an individual to be more gifted then he, therefore his need to rid himself of David's legacy. However, this gifted warrior, David, who slayed a giant, did not choose to even attempt to slay Saul.

David succeeded in almost everything he tried and was respected throughout the land. However, he remained humble even to the extent of not using his popularity against Saul. Even when Saul was on hot pursuit of David, David never allowed pride or arrogance to drive his fear to retaliation. David's love for God placed his honor for Saul ahead of all his fears of Saul and torment by Saul. Instead of taking matters into his own hands at this time David cries out to the Lord, "I come to you for protection, O Lord my God. Save me from my persecutors, rescue me!" (Psalm 7:1). Not only does he cry out to the Lord for protection, but also when David has the opportunity to kill Saul, end all the torment, he chooses not to.

The first time he chose to spare Saul's life was in a cave that David was hiding and Saul came in to "relieve himself". Unbeknownst to Saul, David was right there; close enough to cut a piece of Saul's robe. So instead of cutting Saul's throat, David cut his robe stating, "The Lord forbid me that I should do this to my lord the king. I shouldn't attack the Lord's anointed one, for the Lord himself has chosen him" (1 Samuel 24:6). David's fear and respect for his Lord far outweighed his fear of his lord, the king. I find that amazing. Saul clearly torments David. Saul is clearly driven crazy by his own jealousy of David. David has been chased out of his hometown and on the run for his life. Saul is relentlessly pursuing him for no other reason than David is honorable and strong, and yet, David spares Saul's life.

Not only does David spare Sauls life but he says to Saul, "I will never harm the king, he is the Lord's anointed one……May the Lord judge between us. Perhaps the Lord will punish you for what you are trying to do to me, but I will never harm you" (1 Samuel 24:9-15). I cannot imagine how hard it would be to have this face off with a crazed enemy, knowing I have the power to take their life but instead give them honor. This humble stance of David's speaks to me on so many levels. I love that David has such a strong relationship with the Lord that he first KNOWS beyond a shadow of a doubt that his Lord will rescue him in due time;

> Hear me as I pray, O Lord. Be merciful and answer me! My heart has heard you say, "come and talk with me." And my heart responds, "Lord I am coming." Do not turn your back on me. Do not reject your servant in anger. You have always been my helper. Don't leave me now; don't abandon me, O God of my salvation! Even if my father and mother abandon me, the Lord will hold me close. Teach me how to live O Lord. Lead me along the right path, for my enemies are waiting for me. Do not let me fall into their hands. For they accuse me of things I have never done; with every breath they threaten me with violence. Yet I am confident I will see the Lord's goodness while I am here in the land of the living. Wait patiently for the Lord. Be brave and courageous. Yes, wait patiently for the Lord. (Psalm 27:7-14).

David talks to God through his Psalms as if he believes God is listening. He speaks to God with such a beautiful level of trust and intimacy that draws me in. His conversations to God are as if he just knows that God is listening, and not only listening but that God will take care of all that is happening. This confidence is first evident when he faces Goliath as a young boy. He says to the towering giant, "You come to me with sword, spear, and javelin, but I come to you in the name of the Lord of Heaven Armies, the God of the armies of Israel, whom you defied" (1 Samuel 17:45). He tells Goliath that he has great assurance of God giving him the victory, "so everyone assembled here will know that the Lord rescues his people, but not with the sword and spear" going on to clarify, "this is the Lord's battle and he will give you to us!" (1 Samuel 17:47).

During his flight from Saul, David continued to live that truth out. David had such a humble stance that he was able to stay true to keeping the perspective that God was in control and that although he had enemies surrounding him he had nothing to fear. David's relationship with the Heavenly Father allowed him to be fearless even when things seemed hopeless. This fearlessness allowed him to be honorable. Honorable even when "the anointed one" was without honor.

David did not allow his fear to drive his choices staying level headed, even when his enemy was within hands reach. David had a second opportunity to kill Saul, when he was given Saul's location. David approached the enemy camp while Saul and his men were sleeping. He came up to Saul, removed his sword and water jug but still chose the high road of no harm. David said to Abishai, "Don't kill him. For who can remain innocent after attacking the Lord's anointed one? Surely the Lord will strike Saul down someday, or he will die of old age or in battle. The Lord forbid that I should kill the one he has anointed!" (1 Samuel 26:9-11). Even at Saul's very worse, David recognized that the Lord still had purpose in Saul being king. David recognized God's authority to place whomever He wanted in authority. David recognized that even though he was innocent, he was being sought out by a mad man, and that this mad man had been allowed by God to take the throne of king.

In knowing and respecting God's full authority to place whom He wanted in authority, David stayed humble waiting patiently on the Lord until He removed the mad man from authority. I find that can be very hard for me. It can be hard for me to remain humble and respectful to those in positions of authority that I do not agree with or respect, let alone who are trying to devour me. David's full trust in the Lord, even when all are against David, his respect for God's will never waiver. So much so, David maintains a respect for those he recognizes as God placing in authority.

Not only did David choose not to cause harm to Saul, a mad man that hunted him relentlessly, but also he grieved his death when Saul died. "David and his men tore their cloths in sorrow when they heard the news. They mourned and wept and fasted all day for Saul and his son Jonathan, and for the Lord's army and the nation of Israel, because they had died by the sword that day" (2 Samuel 1:11-12). No wonder David was a "man after God's own heart" (Acts 13:22). David loved the Lord more than himself. He trusted the Lord more than he gave into his fear. He honored the Lord more than he honored his own life.

Not only did David honor the Lord with his actions, but he honored the Lord with his heart. He grieved the death of a mad man because he recognized the honor God placed upon Saul by placing Saul in a position of honor. Romans 13:1-2 says, "Everyone must submit to governing authorities. For all authority comes from God, and those positions of authority have been placed there by God." David knew this, acted on it, and lived it.

I struggle however on all three accounts. I think sometimes that it is different now, how could God expect me to trust the authority that sit upon the "throne" because of this or that. As if "this or that" is far worse than the "this or that" that someone like David had to contend with. The truth is, I have never had to contend to what David did. I would like to learn to have the faith to conquer a giant when all odds are against me but God is for me. I would like to have the relationship with God that when my enemies surround me I shall not fear. I would like to have the honor that when faced with dishonor I still stand tall and represent humility, trust, and faith in such a way that my love for the dishonorable will be revealed when they fall at the hands of their enemy. I would like to be considered a woman after God's own heart.

Day 13

Faith and Love

Two things I have really been reflecting upon and praying about the last few weeks is the issue of faith and love. Jesus says the greatest of all commandments is to love God and second but equally as important is to love your neighbor as yourself (Matthew 22:38). I think of how Jesus modeled this love by healing the ear of the soldier that was about to take him into captivity (Luke 22:51). He also revealed this love by asking God, his Father, to forgive those who had nailed Him to the cross and were at His feet gambling for His cloths (Luke 23:34). Oh, how I look to my Abba for the ability to love like that, but I find myself falling far too short of even loving those around me who are not my enemy, especially in times of trials and tribulations. Sadly, I find myself succumbing to a self-centered self-pity attitude when life gets tough, and I have become painfully aware that when I am in this mode, I am unable to love others as I should. I'm too busy wallowing in my pain. Yet, Jesus, while hanging upon the cross experiencing pain far beyond what I could even imagine offers a prayer to His Father for those that inflicted the very pain He was experiencing. As I reflect upon this attitude, I am reminded of James' words that state it is in our trials and tribulations that our endurance, character, and faith may grow. James goes on to challenge the reader that what good is faith if ones actions do not show that faith. It is in our love for others, both our neighbors and our enemies, that God is revealed. It is in our reaching out to others that Christ is seen and nowhere can I find that we are only to reach out to others when life is good to us. In fact, I find that it is truly in our own weakness that Christ will lift us up. It is in our times of greatest weakness that we must have faith and show His strength by turning to Him instead of turning within. Therefore, in this day of trials and tribulations, I will rely on my faith and press into my Abba so His love will shine through in spite of my weakness.

Day 14

Faith or Fear

I love singing songs of praise to my Heavenly Father claiming His faithfulness even in times of trouble. As I sing I am reminded of His loving faithfulness declared throughout the Bible. Even when things seemed dire, He delivered in an eternal way. I also love reflecting on His promises in the Bible that remind me that it is in our times of trials and tribulations that our faith is tested. James writes, "Dear brothers and sisters, whenever trouble comes your way consider it an opportunity for joy. For when your faith is tested, your endurance has a chance to grow. So let it grow, for when your endurance is fully developed, you will be strong in character and ready for anything" (1:2-14). The Psalmist repeatedly reveals this type of character. Even when despair and fear has engulfed them, they claim the faithfulness of God. In this praising, they seem to find comfort. Paul writes about realizing how he can find contentment in whatever state he is in. He does this after being beaten, ship wrecked, and facing execution; he seems to lean on a peace that surpasses all understanding and reveals his endurance by finishing the race strong. And Jesus, the son of God, cries out, "'Eli, Eli, Lema sabachtani?', My God My God why have you forsaken me" (Matt 27:46). However, He still truly knows the love of the Father even in the depths of His pain as reveled in His plea, "Father, forgive these people, because they don't know what they are doing" (Luke 23:34). I am comforted by the vulnerability exposed in these passages in spite of the firm faith displayed. It helps me understand that it is part of the human state and not a sign of weakness or a lack of faith when my flesh cries out in fear. It is not a lack of faith when life delivers that which I do not want. It is not a lack of faith when my physical state is overcome with pain. It is not a lack of faith when I am filled with doubt because God did not give me the answer I wanted or events did not play out quit like I had anticipated. It is not a lack of faith when I am overwhelmed with grief when God does not deliver me from death. The truth is in any one of these situations I find James words to be true. Any time the Lord has carried me through a trial in which He allowed my flesh to cry out to Him, I pressed into Him and trusted in His faithfulness in spite of how I felt. Each time this happens, I find my faith and dependence upon Him grows. I am strengthened so I may accept whatever comes my way. For this day and for whatever it may bring, I will not be overcome by fear but instead embrace the fact that God indeed is all knowing, all powerful, and all loving.

Day 15

Faith that is Yielding

James 3:17 states, "But wisdom that comes from heaven is first pure. It is also peace loving, gentle at all times, and willing to yield to others." "Willing to yield to others" jumps out at me. I have been reflecting on what that means in my relationships and why when I fail to yield to others what is standing in the way. I find my desire to be right, my desire to get my own way, or my desire for comfort are the reasons behind my pushing past another's needs rather than my yielding. One day I was reading in 1 Samuel chapters 24 and 25. In chapter 24, David has the opportunity to kill Saul after being tormented by Saul's jealousy. Yet, David yields to the Spirit and resists his desire to rescue himself from Saul's murderess plots against him. David chooses to spare Saul's life. In chapter 25, David resists the prideful urge to kill Nabal after Nabal expressed great disrespect toward David and refused to assist David and his men. David again yielded to a prompting to not succumb to his own devices. I look to the David represented in these chapters and respect a man that can find strength in yielding. I believe it takes far greater strength to yield and is far more respectful to yield than to allow our desires to rule over others. I find that I have a far harder time respecting David later in 2 Samuel 11 when David gives into lust, takes another man's wife (Bathsheba), and plots to have Uriah (Bathsheba's husband) killed. I wonder what can change a man so much that in one time of his life he is able to overcome even his own fear of losing his life as to not to kill his enemy yet later allows his pride and lust to dictate stealing another man's wife and choreographing the death of that man. It seems that maybe David became so pride filled, believing he should have all that he wanted, that he began living a life of taking what he wanted. He ran over others without thinking of how it may affect others. While reflecting on David and his life, I find that it gives a much greater meaning to what James states, "But wisdom that comes from heaven is first pure. It is peace loving, gentle at all times, and willing to yield to others."

Day 16

Faith Unwavering

James writes, "Dear brothers and sisters what's the use of saying you have faith if you don't prove it with your actions?" (James 3:14). In this time of trials and tribulations, I find these words resonate in my ears. As a believer and a follower of Christ, I believe my responses to the trials and tribulations in my life and of this world should be filled with peace and joy. For if I do not emulate a peace and joy that surpasses all understanding, what type of ambassador to Christ am I? If I cannot walk upon this earth facing what all face without radiating the love of Christ, who am I to try to bring others to that love? If I do not believe in the product and adorn myself in His glory, then who will want to buy into what I want to sell? Therefore, for me, I choose this day to walk in the peace and joy that surpasses all understanding and to love others as Christ has loved me.

Day 17

Faith Walk

Do we expect God to be our short order cook? Do we grow discouraged when things do not go quite as we planned? As Christians do we grown and mumble about all our trials and tribulations? James (1:2-4) challenges us to consider it all joy, even in all our trials and tribulations for they grow us strong, building our endurance and character. Paul (1 Thes. 5:16-18) states to always be joyful, being thankful in all circumstances. How could they say such thing when they were in the midst of persecution? Could it be their focus was not on the temporal world but instead on God's eternal promises? I often wonder if we as Christians claim that Jesus took on the punishment for our transgressions, and He died and rose again to secure our eternal position with our Heavenly Father. If that position is in Heaven, then why, as Christians, are we so focused on our current state? Jesus took on great pain and suffering, far more than I can even imagine. Even Paul took on so much more in the areas of trials and tribulations. He was beaten, stoned, imprisoned, ship wrecked, and left for dead many times, yet he states consider it all joy.

It seems to me that maybe Paul's vantage point was far more eternal than mine. The apostles had such a passion for Christ, and they walked in his shoes willing to leave all else behind sacrificing all for the glory of God. It appears through the records of their actions that their life exemplified the glory of God, and they were blessed. Somewhere along the way, we have lost that passion for Christ that drives us to radiate His love and His promises through us. The early apostles brought so very many to Christ through the passion they exhibited, how are we doing currently with that? If we are going around grumbling and bemoaning our current state while openly claiming freedom in Christ, who would be intrigued to come to Him? Does our faith walk truly reveal the glory of God? James warns us "what good is faith if our actions do not show it" when talking about our treatment of others and the use of our words, gossiping, complaining, lying, and putting others down.

I remember within 24 hours of finding out about my husband's death. I had an image of a woman I had watched from afar walking gracefully through the death of her daughter and later her husband. I determined myself to claim God's mercy and grace at that moment so I may walk in the valley of death with the strength of my Father. I admitted and accepted that I missed my David horribly. However, I embraced and was thankful that my David was in a glorious place with my Father experiencing no more pain. His body was completely healed, and he is singing endless praises to our Lord. Regardless of my earthly pain, I found great peace in knowing He was in a better place. I would wake up mornings after losing David and be filled with sorrow and pain. I missed him so much but found that peace that surpasses all understanding in realizing the promise of seeing him again one day. My grief was real and overwhelmed me at times. Of course, I missed my husband. I loved him and missing him was inevitable. That was the temporal reality of losing him, but the eternal truth was I would see him again. I believe that Paul and others must have had their temporal moments, but they shared with us through their writings the eternal truths. Are we doing that for others?

Day 18

Give Him Your Mustard Seed

This weekend I have been contemplating faith as small as a mustard seed. "Jesus told them. 'I tell you the truth, if you had faith even as small as a mustard seed, you could say to this mountain, 'Move from here to there,' and it would move. Nothing would be impossible'" (Matt 17:20). Thinking through the different seasons of life, the different challenges that may come, and the different places we may be in our faith walk, I am so reassured in knowing that no matter what little we have to offer Him, what little faith we can muster up, He can turn it into something exponentially greater. He can take my meager offerings and feed the masses, sleigh giants, and conquer kings. He will take my weakness and make me strong, give me rainbows in the midst of storms and bring me peace in the middle of my turmoil; all He ask of me is to give Him but a seed.

Day 19

He is my Portion

This past Sunday during the worship time in our service we sang a song with the phrase, "I believe You are my portion, I believe You are all I need." As I lifted those words to my Savior, Jesus Christ, I thought do I truly believe this? If Abba removed all from me, stripped it all away, is Christ all I need. Is the portion He offers sufficient? Can I find peace and joy when all has been taken from me? These are very hard questions. Even in the writing of them I ponder is there a risk of challenging my Heavenly Father so much that He would offer me the opportunity to realize the significance of those words? I think of Job and his plight, and I wonder if my response would be much like his. Then I reflect on Christ and what He endured for me. The portion He took to become my portion, to become all I need. Then I realize, I have what Job did not. I have the knowledge of Jesus Christ as my Savior, my Portion.

Day 20

A Time for Everything

Paul writes, "I have learned, in whatever state I am, therewith to be content" (Philippians 4:11). He also encourages us not to worry about anything but instead pray about everything. Jesus said, "But before all this occurs [speaking of His return], there will be a time of great persecution. You will be dragged into synagogues and prisons, and you will be accused before kings and governors of being my followers" (Luke 21:12). It appears to me that we have been duly warned that being a Christ follower does not mean a life without pain and suffering. In fact Jesus said, "If anyone wishes to come after me, he must deny himself, and take up his cross daily and follow me" (Luke 9:23). I find myself in the morning praying to the Lord and asking Him to use me. However, by evening, I am succumbing to the flesh and complaining as to the difficulties of this life. I have been challenged with knowing of the Lord's calling in my life, becoming excited about it. In fact, I find myself telling others of His sweetness in the clarity of the calling, but then once I am overwhelmed by it, I begin moaning about how hard it is. I have been convicted on a number of occasions as to what type of witness I must be only praising my Father when I am sitting comfortably upon His promises while rejecting the totality of His promises. Sometimes it will be hard!

A promise that I can hold to in the hard times, a truth that can sustain me, is that in my weakness His strength is revealed (2 Corinthians 12:8). God will certainly call us to a place that we cannot sustain the pressure on our own. He promises us He will do that. He also promises us that He will not forsake or leave us. He promises that His grace is sufficient. He promises that in Christ all things are possible. I believe that is why He takes us to a place of great discomfort while we are right smack dab in the middle of His will. He desires to take us to the end of our abilities; this is the place that His abilities are realized. He takes us to deep valleys so His assurances can be found. He takes us to insurmountable mountains so His strength can be found. Sadly, I believe that, as Christians, we fail to embrace these moments as true moments of praise. Sadly, we somehow stop claiming Him as almighty and our witness begins to suffer. I must question what is about our belief system that renders us not embracing the realities of life.

These are realities King Solomon wrote about in Ecclesiastes. King Solomon, the wisest of all wrote about the reality that life is full of seasons. He wrote of a time to be born and a time to die, so why as Christians do we ask "why do loved ones have to die". Never once have I asked my Abba why He took my husband eight years ago, my dad several years after, or my mother just months after my dad. He took them because He could. He is the God that gives and takes away. With life comes death, as Solomon states. Therefore, as a Christian, who am I to think that I am so special to escape what is assured, death? What I have that non-believers do not have is the assurances that He is with me in my valley and that I will certainly see my loved one face to face again. I will spend eternity with them singing heavenly praises to our Abba. I believe I am a far better witness to His promises when I claim them all, even when bad things happen, because bad things will happen. How arrogant non-believers must think Christians are when we are baffled at our losses.

I love the fact that God can rescue us from great pain and suffering if He so chooses. For Solomon states, there is a time to kill and a time to heal. I praise Him for all He has rescued us from. I also recognize how disappointing it can be when God does not choose to rescue. Nevertheless, the truth that all things are turned for good means that even when He chooses not to rescue us from a current suffering, it will be turned for good. Even when we cannot see it. That is what true faith is, believing even when not seeing. Because we have such a limited perspective on things, our perspective is temporal. We can have a very hard time realizing an eternal significance, but the true act of faith is knowing good will come even when we do not see it on this side of eternity. What is currently really bad, He will turn for good.

When we work at keeping an eternal perspective, it does not mean that we will not feel pain at losses. The wise king said there is a time to cry and a time to grieve. Grief is a natural God given response to the missing of our loved one. It is not a lack of faith to grieve at the loss. It is not a failure of claiming God's goodness while we grieve His sovereign act of bringing the one we loved into communion with Him while taking them from us. God walks with us in that valley. He understands our pain. He embraces our sorrow. He also offers us great comfort and healing in it. After the healing and the pain has subsided, He offers us seasons of laughter, joy, and dancing.

God carries us through all different seasons in life. In each season, He is growing us, refining us, and using us. God gives us the beauty of spring and new growth or fall with all the vibrant colors. Spring is such a relief after the frigid cold of winter, and fall is so refreshing after enduring the heat of summer. The beauty that is revealed after extreme seasons is a glory beyond explanation. Both in the climate and in my life. It is the passing of the seasons in my life that keeps me from being complacent throughout my life. I have learned to embrace every moment and count all my blessings. Facing all the challenges, losses, trials, and tribulations knowing each one will grow me and that soon this season will pass into a season full of color, new growth, and change. For I have come to know God is good all the time. He is good.

Day 21

Beauty from Ashes

God is the God that gives and takes away. It is hardly a challenge to praise Him amongst our blessings, when He is pouring down upon us great love and security. It does however become a great challenge for me to praise Him in the storm, when it feels like all has been ripped away from me without a warning. There have been many times throughout my life that things did not go quite as planned and in fact went in a completely opposite direction. I have experienced many a disappointment, some for which I was not so certain I would survive. However, through it all God has truly grown me and made me stronger in Him. As I look back on all the losses, disappointments, and valleys of my life, there was soon to follow a mountain top experience, one that was beyond all expectation and understanding.

One great mountain top came with much a fight from me. After my husband, David, died the Lord quickly started directing me to an unfamiliar land. I felt much like Abraham, leaving my family, my career, everything I knew to go to a faraway land that had many promises. Truly, however, the move was not so hard. It was crazy in so many ways, but I completely knew God was in it. He held me so close during those first few months of David's passing that it just seemed exactly like Him to uproot me from Nacogdoches, Texas and move me to Lynchburg,

Virginia. In many ways, I was excited to see what God would do in my life. I knew I still had much grief to process through, but that would happen weather I was in Nacogdoches or Lynchburg. I knew that was between the Lord and me. He was certainly wherever I was, so I packed up everything I owned, and my daughters and I moved to Lynchburg six months after David died. That was an easy yes.

My first two years in Lynchburg was blessed with quiet time with the Lord, growing new Godly friendships, experiencing new adventures, and letting go of what was no longer in my life. I was settling into a very comfortable routine, enjoying my friends, my new hobbies, spending time with my girls, and traveling. I was comfortable and safe in my current state of singleness. I missed David so much, but I was realizing my life was still very full of wonderful new things God was showing me. I stayed quit secure in the cocoon that I had created until God started tugging at my security and comfort. God started putting on my heart that He wanted me to meet a man that had lost his wife around the same time I lost David. I did not know this man. I just knew of him. I did not want a man in my life, and I certainly was not going to go out seeking some strange man just because I started obsessing about him. At least, that is what it felt like. This man was heavy on my heart. It was as if I was burdened for him.

I did what any good Christian woman would do, whose heart is broken for another. I began praying for this man, and begging God to give this man a Godly woman to love him as his wife did. I did specify with the Lord that this Godly woman would *not* be me. The more I prayed, the more burdened I became. I begged God to bring him a woman soon. I begged God to release my burden of him. I begged God to help me stop thinking of this man I did not know. I felt crazy. I just wanted to get past this obsession. I told no one of my thoughts, fears, or obsessions for surely they would know I had gone over the deep end. This went on for six months with no relief, it almost seemed as though the harder I tried, the more I thought of this man. Finally, I "told" God that if He wanted me to meet this man He would have to divinely intervene. I certainly was not going to tell anyone about any of this. Within two weeks God did just that. He arranged for me to be at the same place Don Brooks, the man, was going to be. I was completely awestruck. Later, I did find out as hard as I was praying against this meeting, there were many that were praying for it.

After meeting Don, my first thought was, "wow he is really handsome." After talking to him for a few minutes, I thought, "he is really nice and funny". I was so very afraid and uncomfortable. I so very much wanted to run. For the next six months, I struggled like I never have before. I fought and pleaded with God not to do this to me again. I was so very afraid of giving my heart to another man to just be broken and left alone one more time. With my first husband leaving me and my second husband dying on me, I just did not want to go through another broken heart. I found it ironic how easy it was for me to just two years prior leave everything I knew and loved to go to a strange place and start a new life. Yet, opening my heart again to love, that seemed impossible. In my struggles, I explained to God all the reasons this would not work. I reminded Him of the things about me that just were not conducive for yet another marriage. I begged him to allow me just to be friends with Don. The struggles and the pain continued until I released my heart to the Lord and told Him to do what He wanted with me.

Don and I did fall in love. Our kids mixed well. Our families embraced the idea of marriage, and we married within the next year. God has taken two broken families and woven us together to make a beautiful tapestry of old and new. My life with Don has been such an incredible blessing. Within the three years of marriage, we have been to Greece two times, Italy, Israel, Bermuda, Bahamas, snow skiing, kayaking, canoeing, hiking, been to Broadway shows, and just enjoyed pleasant evenings out on our deck. We love our time together and embrace God's love. We talk about our loved ones that are no longer with us, and praise our Heavenly Father for rising beauty from the ashes. I am grateful God did not answer my prayers and that I submitted myself to His will.

Day 22

Believing with My Heart what I Profess with My Mouth

Romans 10:9 states, "If you confess with your mouth, 'Jesus is Lord', and believe in your heart that God raised him from the dead, you will be saved." What sticks out at me in that verse is "if I confess and believe with my heart." When I think about that, I am reminded of the challenge James poses, "So you see, faith by itself isn't enough. Unless it produces good deeds, it is dead and useless" (James 2:17). I am challenged in this life to walk out that which I say I believe. Sometimes that is easy but most of the time that is very hard. When I feel slighted, I want to hold a grudge. When I see wrong, I want to judge. When I feel pushed, I want to push back. However, what I confess to believe is that Jesus is Lord of Lord, King of Kings, and that He came upon this earth to wash us all clean of our transgressions. I am told to forgive as He forgives me, that judgment is His and I am to love others as He loves me, and that as He humbly walked and yielded, I am to yield. So today, as I confess with my mouth that Jesus is who He said He was, I will not be overcome by my fears, insecurities, or hurts. For I know the war is already won. I am saved, and any trial or tribulation I might be in the midst of, He will use it for His glory. Therefore, I go confidently maintaining my composure while humbly walking upon this earth proclaiming that which I believe.

Jesus came to conquer death and I have nothing to fear.

Day 23

Do I love Him as He loved me?

I have often reflected upon Jesus' words, "Father forgive them", as He was dying on the cross. Amazing to me is His love for me. It overwhelms me and makes me realize how undeserving I am. Today, I was thinking of how fickle I am about my love and commitment to my Heavenly Father and Savior in spite of His unwavering love for me. I pondered through the last several months and found myself frustrated, sad, confused, and disgruntled at all my life events that have transpired. However, as I sat thinking through why I felt the way I did, I realized I felt that way because I had anticipated things to work out differently than they did. At every turn or bend in the journey the Lord has taken me down since April, I anticipated one outcome and instead got a different outcome. This anticipation had nothing to do with the promises the Lord gave me. It had to do with what I had hoped to happen, my interpretation of what I wanted. Therefore, my frustration, confusion and disgruntled attitude really has everything to do with my poor interpretation of how the journey ended. I misinterpreted the pieces of the puzzle, the backdrop of the road, and the dots in the mural. The full picture only comes when I pull away from the individual events, the moments in time that made me stop and take notice, and instead focus on the significance each moment has to the big picture, the one of eternity. Only then can I realize how God kept every promise He has ever given me. He has poured His love upon me in such an abundance that it takes my breath away. He has answered every prayer spoken or unspoken. I just must look at it through the lens of eternity and not the temporal goggles I have been using. When I look through to eternity and see God in all His greatness, I once again find a love for Him that is beyond anything I can explain. It is just like the love He has for me. It is beyond anything I can explain.

Day 24

Doubt

The last two days I have read of two, John the Baptist and Peter, who faced doubt because of their circumstances. Yesterday my reading was on John the Baptist (Luke 7:18-23) when he sent his disciples to ask Jesus, "Are you the messiah we have been expecting or should we keep looking?" I really do not blame dear John for doubting. He was imprisoned because of his warnings of the coming messiah. I would be also thinking, if I am right about who you are then why is this happening to me. Today I read of Peter (Matthew 14:28-31) when Jesus was walking on the water and he said, "Lord if it is really you then tell me to come to you walking on the water".

On my run this morning, I began reflecting on how much I needed those passages. How often I doubt sovereignty of where I am because of what is happening. My expectations are that if I am in the will of God then all things will be good. There is nothing farther then the truth. In fact, Jesus warned that following Him would not be easy and persecution would come. He lived that truth out, so why should I think I would not have trials and tribulations. Why do I focus on the circumstances around me rather than the God above me?

After Peter asked Jesus to tell him to come, Jesus said, "Yes come." Therefore, Peter did. I often tell the Lord,

"Here am I Lord, send me" and He does. However, just like Peter, I often take my eyes off Him who is in heavenly places and place my sights on that which is around me. When I do that, I, like Peter, begin sinking in the sea of doubt. However, my Jesus is always there saying, "Why do you doubt me? Keep your eyes set on me and all things are possible." So today, I chose not to doubt but to keep my eyes focused on the maker of heaven and earth.

Day 25

Doubt and Fear

Peter's doubt and fear are revealed when he tells Jesus "Heaven forbid, Lord, this will never happen to you" (Matthew 16:22) in response to Jesus' explanation of His impending suffering and death. Peter, like I, was only seeing things from a human perspective and completely missed the fact that Christ told him He would be back. Peter missed the greatest gift, the gift of eternal life, because of his fear and doubt. Jesus rebuked Peter, "Get away from me, Satan! You are a dangerous trap to me. You are seeing things merely from a human point of view, and not from God's" (Matthew 1:23). I can relate to Peter. How many times will I question, test, and doubt my Heavenly Father, disregarding all the fervent promises He has made and kept to me in my lifetime? How many times will I view things through my human lenses rather than through heavenly promises? His word says, "Be anxious for nothing." Yet, I continue to be fearful. This fear clearly keeps me from the "peace I give you" by denying His fervent love for me displayed by His promises that I continually doubt.

Day 26

Entitlement

Friday I was flying to Texas to visit my mother and upon landing for the first leg of the flight, a man in the front chose to delay all behind him while angrily speaking to the steward about his displeasure with a new policy that had inconvenienced him. As I stood behind him waiting until he was done letting the steward know his displeasure, I took note of the stewards reaction. She was kind, courteous, and patient while other passengers behind me were growing impatient with the delay caused by this man's diatribe. I was reminded once again what an entitled being we all are, believing for some reason that we are underserving of anything that may cause us an inconvenience.

We believe we are so undeserving that we will spend time allowing others the opportunity to hear of our right for comfort, even if we are causing another discomfort while we are claiming our own. I find myself to behave very similar to that man at times and it grieves me. I am overwhelmed at knowing that Jesus, the King of Kings, Lord of Lords, my savior who had all the rights to claim entitlement, chose to come and wash His disciple's feet. Not only did He willingly wash their feet, He washed the feet of His betrayer, Judas. In addition, He went willingly to the cross for me. I am brought to tears knowing He did that for me, in spite of me, and am reminded that all He asks in return is for me to love others as He has loved me.

Day 27

Fellowship and Unity

I have been reflecting on God's word and the significance it places on unity of the Church. I also have been drawn to the importance it gives to fellowshipping with one another. I have been impressed time and time again at how busy we are as a people and how little time we have for one another. Just this week I have found myself so busy that I have not had time to sit and reflect long enough to write a devotional. I have found these devotionals have spoken to many of my students and helped them feel connected to the larger body, the class, the school, other believers, and sometimes even to God. Yet, I have been too busy to sit down and write/fellowship with my online family. I have been too busy to fellowship to help bring unity.

This past week I have had several opportunities to sit with other believers as we discussed challenging, hot topics. I have found myself walking away from many a meeting feeling a heaviness and have had to ask myself what that is about. When I reflect back on these meetings, I come to realize the central focus is everyone trying to get everyone else to see the issue in one way or another. It is as if we are so busy arguing our side that we are not hearing each other. It does not feel much like fellowship. It feels more like people coming together trying to convince one another that their position is correct. Walking away from the gathering leaves more of a reflection of hostility, quarreling, and outbursts of anger rather than love, peace, joy, kindness, and self-control. The patience for one another seems scarce while the opinions given seem harsh. What disturbs me most about it is I am right in the middle of it, speaking strongly of my opinion as if it weighs heavier than another's.

I hate it when I walk away from my brothers and sisters feeling that way. It makes me feel so divided from them and so disconnected. My spirit becomes troubled, and I cannot help but to wonder if it is troubled because the truth is we are not meant to be this way with one another. I maybe am not so troubled because you do not see things the way I do, but I am troubled because we are so divided. Divided is defined as separate and apart. We were not created to be apart from one another. We were created to be as one, united, "a state of forming a complete and pleasing whole…..a thing forming a complex whole" (dictionary). Galatians 6:26, "Let us not become conceited, or provoke one another, or be jealous of one another" and Ephesians 4:2 says, "Always be humble and gentle. Be patient with each other, making allowance for each other's faults because of your love. Make every effort to keep yourselves united in the spirit."

It is not a wonder I walk away from such meetings so unsettled. The Spirit that dwells within me is unsettled because that is not the way it should be. Sadly, I have been interpreting the unsettledness as if it is because I need to get others to see things the way I do. In believing that, it causes me to become more passionate about my position, which causes me to move farther and farther away from God's position. I am not reflecting His fruits and more exhibiting my flesh. In moments like this, there is not unity only a great divide. The devil is all in the division, distorting it all, for he has come to kill, steal, and destroy. He does not have final victory, but it certainly seems as though he does have a strong hold on the Body. It seems to me as if the devil has created such an incredible division amongst God's people that we spend more time arguing about issues than loving each other. This has become so epidemic within the Church that we are looking more and more as if we are a collective part of the world and not a separate body united as one. We are to be a pleasing complex whole that is reflective of love, peace, joy, goodness, gentleness, kindness, patience, self-control and faithfulness. It is not a wonder the fellowship is lacking and the business is abundant.

The word "complexity" cannot easily be defined. Ironically, it is too complex of a word to clearly define it as stated in Wikipedia. Overall, it is best defined as something with many parts that interact with each other in multiple ways. There is a definite complexity to the integral parts of a body of believers. We are complex beings and to become of like mindedness and united creates a great challenge, a great complexity. However, as Priscilla Shirer says, "Unity does not mean sameness it means oneness in purpose."

We are already likeminded in purpose, to further the Kingdom. We have a common belief. Jesus, the son of God and born of a virgin birth, came to walk upon this earth to show us how to love one another and to die on the cross. He bore the weight of our sin and took our punishment, so we may be fully and completely forgiven. He did this so that we will be with Him one day on heaven. As Christians, we can come together and stand firm upon that truth. For it is the belief of that very truth that makes us Christian. It becomes very complex after that. It can be very challenging to sit with one another trying to navigate our own understanding of different issues. Navigating these waters can often times lead to a self-sufficiency, a determination that my own understanding of a certain topic is the truth instead of my understanding of *the* Truth. The devil then comes in and begins the division by placing one's opinion against another's opinion. Therefore, the war begins within the body, each small group believing their way is the best way instead of coming together as a body and looking to the head of the body, Christ. We spend more time arguing against each other rather than praying with each other. We spend more time expressing our opinions about the source rather than going to the Source.

I wonder what would happen if we stopped arguing with each other about our positions and instead started praying with each other asking God His position. I wonder what would happen if we stopped trying to convince one another of our rightness and instead started trusting God in His goodness. I wonder what would happen if we stopped convicting each other about the positions taken and loved one another for the position God has given. I wonder what would happen if we stopped attending so to the speck in each other's eyes and gave the log in our own eye to God to remove. I wonder what would happen if we became more God centered and far less me centered. I wonder what would happen if we stopped attending to the importance of sameness of opinion but more focused on the oneness of purpose. Would we then become a strong body of believers that loved God first while loving others as we walked upon this earth? Would we not be a part of this world but really a light to the world? Would we be living in such a way that was truly different and set apart? I just wonder.

Day 28

God Calls us to be Relational Not Reactive

I blogged yesterday pleading with my brothers and sisters to be compassionate for our family, to God's people, warning that the world is watching and reminding all that we are to be ambassadors of Christ. I have been spending time reading through the Gospel of John and have been moved by how the Pharisees were so concerned with the laws of God that they missed the love of God. They were so busy defending what they believed to be important that they completely missed what was most important. They were so busy stating their position in God that they missed Jesus' position of God. They missed the truth for making so much noise with their rhetoric.

Jesus criticized the Pharisees by saying, "practice and obey whatever they tell you, BUT don't follow their example. For they don't practice what they teach……what sorrow awaits you teachers of religious law and Pharisees. Hypocrites! For you shut the door of the Kingdom of Heaven in people's faces." (Matthew 23:2-36). I must ask myself, when I respond to someone with hostility and divisiveness, am I essentially shutting the door to God's Kingdom by not revealing God's love? If I spend all my time pointing to sin in another, have I covered up the love of a forgiving Father and the sacrifice of our Savior on my own sin?

Jesus called the leaders of Religious law hypocrites because they were so busy teaching the law they did not follow in love. Jesus called us to be salt and light to the world and stated "let your good deeds shine out for all to see, so that everyone will praise your heavenly Father" (Matthew 5:14). He later said, "You have heard the law that says, love your neighbor and hate your enemy. BUT, I say, love your enemies! Pray for those that persecute you! In that way you will be acting as true children of your Father in heaven. ….if you love only those who love you what reward is there for that?...if you are kind only to your friends how are you different from anyone else." (Matthew 5: 43-47). Are we acting like true children of God when we are hostile to our brothers and sisters who stand in a different position as us? Are we acting as true children of God when we speak with great hostility about those we perceive as our enemy?

I was moved in reading John, Chapter 5, at how much we as God's church have been acting like the Pharisees and how Jesus spent a lot of time rebuking the Pharisees as compared to gently addressing the sinners. He gently says to the man he healed, "Now you are well; so stop sinning, or something even worse might happen" (John 5:14). He later says, "I tell you the truth, those that listen to my message and believe in God who sent, me have eternal life. They will never be condemned for their sins, but they have already passed from death to life" (John 5:24). However, he goes on to really address the Pharisees and their hostility to those who are not following the law, "you search the scriptures because you think they give you eternal life. But the scriptures point to me! Yet you refuse to come to me to receive this life.......For you gladly honor each other, but you don't care about the honor that comes from the one who alone is God" (John 5:31-47). Jesus spoke more of the need to love others, show compassion, stop pointing fingers, and serving others than He did about following the law.

Jesus' message was about the reality of who He was and is. The reality of who he was and who He is comes from accepting that He came upon this earth to show us how to love others, even our enemies or those that see things differently than us. He came upon this earth to take the sins of the world and receive the full wrath of God to forgive all the sins of this world. He came to tear down the veil that The Law kept up so we could go faultless before our Father and receive His love. He came to this world to show us, His followers, how to love those of this world while not being of this world. He gave His life so others could have life. He invited us to do the same. He invited us to become a part of His living body. Are we doing it when we are standing firm in our divisive position while spouting hostility to those who do not stand with us?

Romans 12:5 states, "so it is with Christ's body. We are many parts of one body, and we all belong to each other." Sadly, we as a body of believers have become very divided and we are beating each other up. Paul reminded us that just as our body has many parts so does the body of believers. We have many parts and many different gifts called in many different directions, and we are called to "bless those who persecute you. Don't curse them; pray that God will bless them. Be happy with those who are happy and weep with those who weep. Live in harmony with each other. Don't be proud to enjoy the company of ordinary people. Don't think you know it all!" (Romans 12:14-16). Who are we to determine that the position someone else is taking is not of the Spirit, a member of the body called in that direction? How are we to know that God's heart is not breaking the hearts of others in different ways, speaking of what He sees as great injustices or the twisting of what He would have for us? Who am I to say that my Abba, our Abba, is not leading the person defending immigrants, standing firm against objectification of women, speaking loud for peace and against gun control, or any other current divisive issue that arises? What if the perspective they are coming from is just a different perspective of our same God who loves us all and is asking us all to stand firm for injustice and to love both our neighbor and our enemy? Who am I to think my perspective is the only right perspective?

It seems as though we, as a body of believers, are behaving far more like the Pharisees with our spiritual pride believing we have the answer and disregarding our brothers' and sisters' answers. Jesus came, showed us how to love, showed us how to be humble, and left saying He would leave us with a gift that would allow us to do even greater than He (John 14:16). Hence, we are given the ability to behave far better than we have been. Jesus, through the approval of our Abba, left us the Holy Spirit whose fruits are love, peace, joy, goodness, kindness, gentleness, patience, self-control, and faithfulness. When we allow the fruits of the spirit to radiate from us, it is then that we are the salt and light for all the world to see the love of the Father.

However, the hostility and division that is evident throughout our responses to this recent election and all the dividing factors has nothing to do with the love of our Father, the salvation found in Christ, nor the power of the Spirit. The hostility and rhetoric continuing in social media and pointed at the body is nothing but self-abusive behavior to the body. It is destroying the body and aborting the purpose of Christ. Paul warned "Let all who are spiritually mature agree on these things. If you disagree on some point, I believe God will make it plain to you" (Philippians 3:15).

 I too believe that God is far bigger than any disagreement we have as a body of believers. I believe we can be overcomers and become victorious if we take our battle position on our knees. Instead of beating each other up with our rhetoric, may we join hands and go to our knees asking the Holy Spirit to unite us where we are divided. Let us pray that we start trusting our Father to give us clarity and direction. God's greatest desire is to have a relationship with us and for us to relate to others. God calls us to love others as He loves us. Our God is a relational God and invites us into a relationship with Him. Through Christ, God revealed to us how we are to relate to others. Are we truly relating to others? Or are we reacting to others?

Day 29

God's Masterpiece

Last weekend my twin grandbabies were born. The circumstances were not perfect. They were a month early and my daughter was in a medical crisis. Therefore, the doctors made the choice to deliver the precious angels early. My little Barry weighed a little over 4 pounds, and precious Finleigh weighed almost 6 pounds. They looked so very little in the incubators, and little Finleigh looked so very frail hooked up to the breathing machine. However, what stood out to me were how perfect their little bitty hands were and the perfect formation of their ears. I just could not believe how flawless they looked even at their little size. I thought immediately of Psalm 139:14 where David writes, "you made all my delicate, inner parts of my body and knit me together in my mother's womb." I thanked God for how carefully He formed them, so much so that they were going to survive this early arrival. It was a miracle to me, seeing the precious little beings knowing only God could create something so awesome and beautiful. I then looked at the IV's in their little arms and all the tubes and wires they were hooked up to. I heard Finleigh cry as the nurses did what they needed to do, and I thought how cruel the world must seem to her. Just hours ago, she was nestled safe in her mother's womb only to literally be yanked out in to the big harsh world.

I prayed that neither she nor Barry would allow the things

of this world to cause them to forget they are the "workmanship" of our wonderful creator (Psalm 139:14). I thought how easily I forget that I too am fearfully and wonderfully made in His image. In my forgetfulness, I allow the things of this world to weigh me down. Sometimes, the harshness of this world can overwhelm me to the point of forgetting who my creator is, one that knit me perfectly in my mother's womb so that His glory can be realized through my life. Oh, how I want that for all four of my grandchildren, Raeligh (3), Rueben (1), and Barry & Finleigh (newborns), but first maybe I must emulate that in my life forging a pathway to a reckless abandonment to the Holy One, my Creator.

Day 30

He Washed Their Feet

Jesus was facing His final hours, and He knew the death He was about to face. Yet, He washed the feet of the disciples. He did not run. He did not riot. He did not point fingers or speak badly of those who were rioting, running, pointing fingers or opposing Him. Instead, He washed the feet of the disciples, a custom that was left to the servants of the household. Yet, Jesus, our Savior, washed the feet of His disciples in His final hours. He washed the feet of Peter knowing Peter would deny Him three times. What is even more compelling is that Jesus washed the feet of His betrayer, Judas, knowing he would turn Jesus over to His enemies. Jesus washed their feet instead of convicting or condemning them to hell; in fact, He went to the cross to spare them eternity in hell. After washing their feet, He said, "I am giving you a new commandment: Love each other. Just as I have loved you, you should love each other. Your love for one another will prove to this world that you are my disciples" (John 13:34-35). Jesus came so He could show us how to love others. He came so the world could see who we belonged to. Jesus came so He could show us how to be light to others and so others may come to recognize the light. I must ask myself, how well am I washing the feet of others and loving them as Christ loved me? How well am I loving those who deny me? How well am I loving those deny my significance or even betray me?

SITTING WELL AT THE WELL

How well am I shining the light of love into this dark world? Or am I just sitting in the dark, adding darkness by spouting off at those who oppose me and attacking those who betray me?

DR. JEANNE BROOKS

In Closing

The Neurobiology of Spiritual Warfare

Dr. David Jeremiah has a great book, *The Spiritual Warfare Answer Book*. In it, He clearly explains the tactics of the devil and the strategic way the devil has to steal, destroy, and kill. Dr. Jeremiah quotes John Phillips, "But our real enemy lurks in the shadows of the unseen world, moving people as pawns on the chessboard of time. As long as we see people as enemies and wrestle with them, we will spend our strength in vain." The devils main purpose or goal is to destroy our witness and to render us useless in furthering God's eternal Kingdom. God calls us to love one another as He loves us. He calls us to be anxious for nothing but prayerful and thankful for all things....setting our mind on His truths and His love (Philippians 4:6-9).

Paul writes in Galatians 5 that we are not to become conceited, provoke one another, or be jealous of one another. He talks about the fruits of the Spirit: peace, joy, love, goodness, gentleness, kindness, patience, self-control and faithfulness. However, he also warns us against the sinful nature of mankind and stating that hostility, outbursts of anger, selfish ambition, dissension, division, and envy are just a few of the realities that we are acting outside of how God would have us behave. I find it poignant that the devils ways of using us as pawns in his warfare is through deceit, divineness, and destruction.

The devil destroys our ability to exhibit the fruits of the

Holy Spirit when he uses us as pawns causing us to wrestle with others. All it takes is one word out of context to trigger one's insecurities, pride, or self-righteousness. The devil is a very crafty enemy. He has been studying us, and he knows our vulnerabilities. He is lurking in the dark just waiting to use someone to pounce upon our pride or our shame so we may be reactive. In addition, reactivity triggers reactivity. We are prone to react to one another. That is why the Bible is so explicit on how not to be reactive. The Bible gives us warning after warning. "Be slow to anger, slow to speak quick to listen." "Be still and know I am God." "Be directed by the Spirit." "Be humble and gentle." "Make every effort to keep united by the Spirit." "Be kind to each other, tenderhearted, forgiving one another, just as God through Christ has forgiven you." These are just a few from Paul's writings. There are many more throughout the Bible from Old Testament, Psalms, Proverbs and New Testament. Proverbs is full of warnings against pride and speaks clearly of how we are to be to one another.

God has many warnings and guidelines for us to be with one another so we can be witnesses to His glory, His love, and His perfect plan for us. God gave us Jesus Christ. He allowed Jesus to walk amongst us to show us how to love one another, be slow to speak, slow to anger, and be humble. We are asked, as Christ followers, to behave in such a manner and not to succumb to the trappings of this world so we may witness to the ends of the world. God requires us to be set apart from things of this world. He warns us not to grow anxious and not to be prideful. It is in the act of doing so that others come to be curious as to what we have they do not. God asks us, requires us, to learn to sit well at The Well. As I wrote in the Neurobiology of Sitting Well, I explained it takes a higher level of intellect to do so.

The devil's ploy is to keep us away from that higher level of intellectual process; the enemy wants to keep us entrapped in our reactive brain, our limbic system. The limbic system is the area of the brain that registers a threat and sets our body in a "go motion" setting us to react. In this reactive mode, there is little room for reason, logic, or emotional regulation. Instead, we are set in a primal place of reacting very quickly to what is perceived as a threat. This area of the brain works very well when there is a real threat. It sets in motion our body to respond very quickly without having to think through what we are doing. Anyone who has come very close to a car wreck has experienced the limbic system at its best.

The problem is our limbic system cannot determine real threat as compared to a perceived threat. It takes the hippocampus and amygdala to help process real as perceived threat. These structures are actually on the outer edges of the limbic system. A well-formed limbic system allows for a level of "slow to anger, slow to speak" while quickly processing real as compared to perceived threats. In essence, God created us in such a beautifully complicated way that we are given the ability, unlike other animals, to relate in a far more relational way by processing external information so we have the capacity to be encouraging and edifying rather than reactive, divisive, and destructive.

However, the devil, our only true enemy, has an ability to wreak havoc on our limbic system. An over active limbic system is an anxious agitated brain. Neurologically speaking, if we are left in our limbic system too long by prolonged exposure to stress, crisis, or trauma, we begin to have a hypersensitive reactive brain. It takes less external stimulation to get us reacting to the outside world. The more reactive we are, the less relational we are. The less relational we are, the more divisive we are. The best way for the enemy to destroy and conquer is by dividing the army, isolating warriors, and creating so much noise that there is mass chaos and mayhem. The devil has done a beautiful job at isolating and dividing the Body of Christ by first causing us to be so busy.

We have become too busy to sit and fellowship. Our churches have become so big that we are lost in the sea of faces and our lives have become so busy we spend very little time sitting with one another. When we are isolated, all we have is ourselves. The body is not working as it should by encouraging one another, lifting one another, and reminding one another of God's goodness and promises. We are not reminding one another of His faithfulness; therefore, we are less inclined to set our mind on what is true about Him. We are then more likely to be drawn into what the world says if true. This Christian walk takes faith, but we begin to lose faith when we are overly focused on the world. We are warned to be in the world but not of it. Yet, the devil has created such a divisive ploy in the body off believers that it is far easier to become overwhelmed by the things of this world.

We find ourselves overwhelmed, anxious, and exhausted, leaving us trapped in our limbic systems, our reactive brain. He then lies to use by making us believe that we are staying connected by social media and electronic communication. He lies to us causing us to believe that this type of interacting is sufficient in cultivating and nourishing relationships. We buy into the lie that we are just too busy to take the time to actually talk to someone, to have a verbal exchange that requires far higher level of intellect rather than the electronic deliverance of information. We have bought into the lie that Facebooking and texting is a sufficient form of communication and can edify the body.

The truth is this form of interacting is literally just a form of basic data processing. This form of interacting is about delivering and retrieving data. It does not really require engagement of the frontal higher cortex that is used in the act of relating and sitting with others. This higher cortex area of the brain helps us grow in our emotional intelligence. Emotional intelligence is what allows us to empathize and relate, truly relate to others and emotional regulate. This area of the brain allows us to be relational not reactive. Empathy allows us to sit with one another, even if we disagree with one another, and listen. It is the ability to place ourselves in another's shoes. It is the ability to see another perspective rather than believing our own perspective is the only truth. It allows us to better walk through conflict without devouring and destroying each other.

However, the enemy wants us to destroy and devour each other. He wants to use us as his pawns, moving us around on the chessboard of life attacking each other "in the name of Christ" so that the world sees us as no different or maybe even worse than the world. The devil is using our limbic system, holding us hostage in our reactive brain, so that we lose our ability to be salt and light to this world.